D1715034

Jokes & More Jokes

compiled by Sandra K. Ziegler
illustrated by Diana L. Magnuson

 CHILDRENS PRESS, CHICAGO

17340

Created by

Library of Congress Cataloging in Publication Data

Ziegler, Sandra, 1938-
  Jokes and more jokes.

  (Laughing matters)
  Summary: A collection of old and new jokes on many
subjects from many countries, with suggestions on
writing your own jokes.
  1. Wit and humor, Juvenile (1. Jokes) I. Magnuson,
Diana, ill. II. Title III. Series.
PN6153.Z53   1983   818'.5402   82-19742
ISBN 0-516-01871-X

TABLE OF CONTENTS

Through the Years

No one knows for sure who told the first joke, or even when it was told. If you closed your eyes and imagined, you would probably get a picture similar to this:

Caveman (to his wife): Now, honey, if you were being chased by a man-eating tiger, what would you do?
Cavewoman: Be glad I'm a woman.

Perhaps you have wondered what kinds of jokes your parents or your grandparents told and laughed at when they were young, or what George Washington thought was funny. Just for laughs, in this chapter you will find some of the kinds of jokes that people have chuckled over through the years.

SETTLING A NEW LAND (1600s)

Faith: Did you know that when you get up in the morning you dress your left foot last?
Charity: No. And I don't believe it's true.
Faith: Of course it is. Whichever foot you dress first, the other is the left one!

AS THE COUNTRY GREW (1700s and 1800s)

Some of the most popular jokes in the early days of our country were exaggerations. They stretched the truth to the point of being outlandish lies. They were called Jonathanisms.

Did you hear about the boy down the block? — He grew so fast his shadow couldn't keep up with him.

Did you hear what people say about Timothy Buttons? — He's so tall he has to get down on his knees to put his hands in his pockets.

MORE JONATHANISMS

My neighbor's feet are so big that when it rains he lies down and uses them for an umbrella.

Jim and Tim are so lazy it takes two of them to sneeze—one to put his head back and the other to say, "Kerchoo!"

SAM WELLER

In the 1830s Charles Dickens invented a character named Sam Weller. For more than 200 years, people have delighted to use a style of humor much like that which Sam Weller used. Certain jokes have come to be known as Wellerisms. A Wellerism often makes use of a pun. It starts in a common way but takes a turn you are not expecting.

WELLERISMS

"I've been framed," the man said when he broke the picture over his head.

"This is a sticky situation," said the teacher when she upset the glue.

"That's the end of my tail," said the cat as he backed into the electric fan.

"I'm down on you," said the man who slipped on the ice and fell on the sidewalk.

"Do you have a book on how to bring up children?" asked the mother whose twins had fallen down a well.

"If you value your life, don't upset me," said the gentleman to his carriage driver.

LITTLE WILLY AND LITTLE AUDREY
(1900-1930)

Little Willy and Little Audrey jokes are the kinds of jokes we still tell and hear someone say, "That's sick." Little Willy/Audrey jokes were patterned after Billy jokes which were popular in England at the same time.

The jokes below come from a book with a title that tells you the kinds of jokes it has. Written by D. Streamer, it is titled *Ruthless Rhymes for Heartless Homes.*

Little Willy rocked the boat.
   He did it as a prank.
   And just to see the bubbles
   That came when Polly sank.

Little Willy hit his ball
   And sent it down the school-
      house hall.
   From a door came Jimmy Bill.
   They say his teeth are missing
      still.

Little Willy pushed poor Kent.
   He landed in the wet cement.
   That gave Willy quite a lift
   To think of Kent when he was
      stiff.

CONFUCIUS JOKES (1930s)

Confucius was a teacher and wise man who gave advice to the Chinese during a troubled part of China's history. When the United States was going through the troubled days of the early part of this century, many gave advice on how to solve its problems. With so many giving advice, it was only natural that humorists should begin to poke fun at the advice-givers. And Confucius jokes were born.

Confucius say: He who puts face in punch bowl will get punch in nose.

Confucius say: He who sticks head through window will get pane in neck.

Confucius say: He who is hit by whale will have cause to wail.

Confucius say: He who sticks head in oven will end up with baked bean.

TOM SWIFTIES (1950s)

Tom Swift was the hero of a series of books. He was a businesslike young man created by the same authors who wrote the Hardy Boys and Nancy Drew books. When a series of books about Tom Swift appeared in the mid-'50s, puns began to appear based on the character in the books. The jokes were called Tom Swifties.

"I'm going to complain to the manager about this cheeseburger," Tom beefed.

"I'm going to take up taxidermy," Tom said, stuffily.

"I'm late for a pressing engagement at the dry cleaners'," Tom said, steaming.

"I loved the Valentine you sent me," Tom said, heartily.

"Tom, you are the only one in the class to get an F," the teacher said, degradingly.

ELEPHANT JOKES
(1960s)

It isn't that people never told elephant jokes before the '60s. They did. Early in the century you probably could have heard an elephant story, but in the '60s a *herd* of elephant jokes passed through.

Do you know why the elephant didn't get rich?—He worked for peanuts.

Did you hear about the elephant who sat on a marshmallow?—He didn't want to fall in the hot chocolate.

Customer: I'll have an elephant float.
Soda Operator: How do you make an elephant float?
Customer: Mix an elephant with ice cream and root beer.

Moe: I can't get my elephant to take a vacation.
Joe: Why not?
Moe: He doesn't like to carry his trunk.

Enough about what others have laughed at over the years. It's time to get on with what's funny today. After all, this may be the very day that you get a chance to tell a joke to someone and brighten his day with a laugh.

A good joke is like potato salad. If you share it with others, you'll have a picnic. Whatever you do, don't be selfish with all the funny things you discover in this book. Pass them on!

If you happen to be someone who has special fascination with dinosaurs, or your family is filled with scientists, you'll like the way this book is arranged. You can go right to the topic of jokes which interest you most and enjoy those first. But whatever you do, don't skip *all* the others.

About Science

First Monkey: Boy, do I have this team of scientists trained.
Second Monkey: How do you mean?
First Monkey: All I have to do is press the buzzer, and one of them gives me something to eat.

Lara: I can't figure it out. Why would a junior scientist stick his finger in the electric socket?
Darcy: That's easy. He wanted to find out about current events.

Astronaut: Did you see the computer programmer?
Technician: She was right here, but she just left.
Astronaut: Which way did she go?
Technician: She went data way.

Did you hear about the archaeologist who took a
supply of dehydrated food to eat while on a
month-long dig?— He got caught in a rainstorm
and gained a hundred pounds before he had time
to get in out of the rain.

Did you hear about the computer expert who
crossed her computer with a rubber band so it
could make snap decisions?

"Which travels faster, heat or cold?" asked the
science teacher.
"Heat," answered the student. "Anybody can catch
cold."

What did the archaeologist say when he fell into the
ancient burial crypt?— I want my mummy!

Scientist to Lab Assistant: Put this box to your ear
and listen.
Lab Assistant: I can't hear anything.
Scientist: I know. It's been like that all day.

Girlfriend: What are you going to do tonight?
Astronomer: I'm going to Hollywood and watch
the stars come out.

The scientist had just lost his grant and he was
  feeling most upset.
"What would you do if you were in my shoes?"
  he asked his colleague.
"Polish them."

Lab Assistant: What is yellow, has black spots, and
  crawls?
Biologist: I give up. What?
Lab Assistant: Whatever it is, it's crawling on your
  shoulder.

About Monsters

Dirk Dragon: Dean, why are you scratching?
Dean Dragon: Nobody else knows where I itch.

Mert: Why do you keep whistling, Perk?
Perk: It frightens the monsters away.
Mert: Don't be silly. We don't have monsters
around here.
Perk: See! It works!

Teacher: What is the difference between a monster
and a peanut butter sandwich?
Student: I don't know, Mrs. Thompson.
Teacher: I'm certainly glad I didn't ask you to pick
up my sandwich.

Maude: How do you keep a zombie from charging?
Claude: Cut up his credit card.

First Witch: This special brew is making my legs
 smart.
Second Witch: Quick! Rub some on your head.

The tiny white ghost walked through the wall and
 floated toward the king's throne. The king's knees
 began to knock.
"Yes?" asked the king, his voice shaking.
"I want to haunt your castle," sighed the ghost.
"By all means, be my ghost," said the king.

First Vampire: I've finally found the right ship for
 me, and I'm going to sea.
Second Vampire: What kind of ship are you going
 on?
First Vampire: A blood vessel.

Mert: What would you do if you had a pet monster
 and he was dying?
Perk: I'd put him in the living room.

First Witch: You can't drive a nail into the wall with
 a broomstick.
Second Witch: Are you sure?
First Witch: Of course, use your head!

Jekyll: What do mummies do on the night of a full moon?
Hyde: They have a wrap session.

Did you hear about Farmer Jones?—He's so smart he put a ghost in his barn so the cows would give milk shakes.

Oceanographer: Do you think there is any truth to the story that the Loch Ness Monster had a banquet?
Diver: I could check his garbage.
Oceanographer: What would a monster have at a banquet?
Diver: Fish and ships, I suppose.

Tom was showing his parents the monster he had made in Art. It had blue skin and a green beard and looked like a first-rate monster.
"What will you do with a blue monster?" asked Mother.
"I suppose," said Tom, "that I will try to cheer him up."

Jekyll: Did you hear that the hobgoblin went to the theater last night?
Hyde: I'll bet that gave the actors stage fright.

Did you hear about the haunted hotel that put in a new elevator?—They wanted to raise their spirits.

Mert: Did you know the Loch Ness Monster never eats chicken?
Bert: Why not?
Mert: Chicken puts him in a fowl mood.

The ghosts were in a special meeting. "Are we all agreed that we must organize ourselves to protect each other from the phantom ships?"
The ghosts agreed.
"Good," said the leader, and they all joined the Ghost Guard.

About Dinosaurs

Caveman: What did the Brontosaurus do when he
  broke his big toe?
Cavewoman: He called a big tow truck.

"What did you name your twins?" one dinosaur
  asked the other.
"Oh," said the proud mother, "they are both Ed."
"Why did you name them both the same name?"
"Because two Eds are better than one."

Did you hear about the Allosaurus that wanted to
  talk to the ocean?—He stood by the sea, but all it
  would do was wave.

"That's the dino doctor," the caveman explained to
his visitor from the far side of the mountain.
"Oh," said the guest, "what does he do?"
"He keeps everyone in stitches."

Did you hear about the baker that mixed up a
dinosaur and a duck?
What did he make?
Dinosaur quackers.

"Come and see Deano, the Dino," said the
caveman's wife. "He isn't himself."
"Why not?" asked the dino doctor.
"He caught a cold and now he's a little hoarse."

Cavewoman: Why did the dinosaur chase the horse
off the cliff?
Caveman: He wanted to see a horsefly.

Cavewoman: What does a dinosaur have that no
other reptiles have?
Caveman: Dinosaur babies.

A Tyrannosaurus broke
into the computer
lab and ate a
computer. Now he is
the biggest know-it-
all in the world.

How do you make a dinosaur stew?—Hide his
   pajamas.

Cavewoman: What would I get if I crossed a
   dinosaur and a fly?
Caveman: I don't know.
Cavewoman: I don't either, but if it lands on you,
   you'll be a goner.

Cavewoman: I saw a Brontosaurus eat with his tail.
Caveman: Don't be silly. A Brontosaurus can't
   eat with his tail.
Cavewoman: Of course he can! He can't take it off!

Cavewoman: Did you ever tickle a dinosaur?
Caveman: No.
Cavewoman: Try it, you'll get a kick out of it.

Caveman: What are you doing?
Cavewoman: Telling jokes to the dinosaurs.
Caveman: Why are you doing that?
Cavewoman: So they will die laughing.

How do you make a red
dinosaur float?—Add
strawberry soda, two
scoops of strawberry ice
cream and a dinosaur.

Did you hear about the Brontosaurus who stomped
through the potato field?—He mashed the
potatoes.

"What are you doing?" asked the caveman.
"I'm knitting another sock," said his mate.
"What for?" asked the caveman.
"My pet dinosaur just grew another foot."

Caveman: Whew! That was close. I was out in the
jungle by myself and a dinosaur charged me.
Cavewoman: What did you do?
Caveman: I paid him.

"How can you tell if you have a dinosaur in your
peanut butter sandwich?"
"I don't know," said the cavewoman. "How?"
"His neck will stick out."

Silly Sam and Sally Jokes

Silly Sam and Sally represent the male/female comedy teams that have amused millions with their wit.

Silly Sam: Boy, was I ever in hot water last night.
Sally: You were? What did you do?
Sam: I took a bath!

Silly Sam: My dog got into the pantry and ate a whole clove of garlic.
Sally: How is he?
Sam: I'll say this much—his bark is worse than his bite.

Sally: How was school today, Sam?

Silly Sam: It was fun. Tomorrow I have to take a holster and a toy gun.

Sally: For Show and Tell?

Sam: No. Teacher said tomorrow she's going to teach us to draw.

Sally: How did you like the play last night?

Silly Sam: I only got to see the first act. I didn't get to see Act Two.

Sally: Oh, why not?

Sam: The program said: Act Two—Six Months Later. So I went home.

Sally: I bet you don't know how books are like houses.

Sam: Sure I do; they both have stories.

Sally: What's the difference between a cake and a plaster cat?

Silly Sam: I don't know.

Sally: I'm sure glad I didn't send you to pick up my birthday cake.

Silly Sam: I'm going to cross a galaxy with a toad.
Sally: You better not. You'll be sorry.
Sam: Why?
Sally: Don't you know what you'll get?
Sam: No. What?
Sally: Star Warts.

Sally: If you eat the rest of the ice cream, you'll
burst.
Silly Sam: Okay. Pass the ice cream and duck.

Sally: That's an interesting pair of socks you have
on, Sam. One brown and one green.
Sam: You really like them? I have another pair at
home just like them.

Sally: How far down do you want to sit?
Silly Sam: All the way, of course.

Sally: Sam, Mom wants you to run across the street and see how old Mrs. Wilcox is.
Sam: Okay.
Mom to Sam: Well, what did she say?
Sam: She says it's none of your business how old she is.

Sally: Did you know there was a kidnapping down the street?
Sam: No? Really?
Sally: Yes, but his mother woke him up.

Silly Sam: I think I'm going to be a secret agent for the CIA when I grow up.
Sally: Oh, what makes you think that?
Sam: I have a code in my head.

Sally: Dad said I can play with the sled half the time.
Silly Sam: Okay. You can have it going up the hill and I'll have it coming down.

Sally: Did you give the goldfish some fresh water today?
Silly Sam: Don't be silly. They haven't finished the water they had yesterday.

Silly Sam: Did you hear? Sweet Charity had her foal last night.
Sally: Oh, tell me about it.
Sam: It's a night mare.

Silly Sam: I wanted to go down to the restaurant, but I guess it's closed.
Sally: What makes you think so?
Sam: The sign in the window says, "Home Cooking."

Sally: Sam, what are you doing pounding on the floor?
Silly Sam: You said it could use some wax.

Puns In Jokes

Two boys were discussing the building going up downtown. "I looked through the holes in the fence," said the first boy.
"They are knotholes," explained his friend.
"They aren't? If they are not holes, what are they?" the first boy demanded.

A farmer is a man outstanding in his field.

Teacher to student: Why would you bring your duck with you to class?
Student: I want him to be a wise quacker.

New Mother: Do you
know what the
difference is between
my baby and
Princess Diana's?
Doctor: No, what?
New Mother: Her baby
is the Prince of Wales
and mine is only the
prince of wails.

Jack had his backpack ready to leave for camp.
"Did you put in some toothpaste?" asked his
mother.
"I don't plan to get in a fight," said Jack, "and my
teeth aren't loose."

Darcy: Do you know those people over on the next
street who live in the lavender house with the
lavender fence?
Lara: They have a boy named Lawrence and he can
lilac anything.

Mother: Sarah, what are you doing to that poor bee?
Sarah: I'm trying to teach it to quilt.
Mother: That's silly.
Sarah: Not if you want to have a quilting bee.

As the tourist said on his first safari in Africa,
"Now that's a real boar!"

Overheard at the turtle races: "Do you know how to make a turtle fast?"
"Of course. Don't give him any food."

Three fishermen were out in a boat. They had four cigarettes but no matches. I have an idea," said one of the fishermen. He threw one of the cigarettes into the lake and made the boat a cigarette lighter.

"Why do you keep your fish on the piano?" asked Joan. "Doesn't the sound bother them?"
"Oh, no," said Kathy. "They are piano tunas."

Sergeant: Why is the captain letting that rookie cop assign the men to their beats?
Second Sergeant: The rookie told the captain he used to live on a farm and he'd had a lot of experience picking beets.

From Many Countries

ENGLAND
Elizabeth: Will you join me
in a cup of tea?
Mary: Yes, but do you think
we will both fit?

CANADA
Doris: How did the quarrel you had with LuAnn
come out?
Morris: She came to me on her hands and knees.
Doris: She did? What did she say?
Morris: Come out from under that bed, you coward.

BELGIUM
Henri: What do you think of your new sister?
Adriene: I can tell you, we needed a lot of things
around the house more!

SCOTLAND
Alexander: I bet I know what you're going to say
next.
George: What?
Alexander: See, I knew you'd say what.

URUGUAY
Rico: Grandma, do you have the kind of glasses that make things look bigger?
Grandma: Yes, Rico.
Rico: Would you take them off and cut me a piece of cake?

WALES
Doctor: Did you remember to follow the instructions for using the medicine I gave you?
Jane: You mean to drink water 30 minutes before I went to bed?
Doctor: Yes.
Jane: I tried, but in 8 minutes I was too full to drink another drop.

PHILIPPINES
Juan Tamad is so lazy he walks his dog under a rose bush so he won't have to scratch his pet.

AUSTRIA

Mayor: Do you know why our cow wears a bell?
Tourist: No. Why?
Mayor: Her horns don't work.

FINLAND

Kauko: You don't write very fast. What are you writing?
Wendy: I'm writing to my brother, and he can't read very fast.

SAUDI ARABIA

Teacher: Why are you shivering, Khalid? It's not cold in here.
Khalid: It must be the zero on my math paper.

RUSSIA

Tasya: Hello, I'd like to speak to the principal, please. Yes, Mr. Youssef. Tasya Wittkopf won't be able to come to school today. She has a toothache.
Mr. Youssef: May I ask who is calling, please?
Tasya: This is my mother.

INDIA

Student: Why did Kumar bring a gun to the basketball game?
Fellow Student: The coach told him that tonight he would finally get to shoot the ball.

UGANDA
Zesiro: What is a student who didn't study most likely to say?
Kizza: I don't know.
Zesiro: Correct.

JAPAN
Kiyoshi: Look at my invention. It will let you look through a wall.
Ringo: That's great. What do you call it?
Kiyoshi: A window.

AFRICA
Simba: Doctor, something is wrong with my dog. He keeps going around in circles.
Doctor: Don't worry. He's a watchdog and he's just winding himself up.

BORNEO
"The next time I'm sick I'm going to a doctor on an outer island," said the patient who was plainly disgusted.
"Why is that?" asked the nurse.
"That doctor is mean," said the patient. "He said he would treat me, but I had to pay for it."

Other Ideas In Jokes

WESTERN BRANDS

Cowboy: That's a splendid painting. What is it?
Dude: It's a steer, eating grass.
Cowboy: Where's the grass?
Dude: The steer ate it.
Cowboy: Where's the steer?
Dude: Do you think he'd stick around after he ate all the grass?

Dude: Can you tell me some uses for cowhide?
Cowpoke: Well, it holds the cow together.

Dude: Look at that bunch of horses in the pasture.
Cowpoke: Herd.
Dude: Of course, you heard.
Cowpoke: No, herd of horses.
Dude: Of course I've heard of horses.
Cowpoke: No! A horse herd.
Dude: I don't care if a horse heard! I don't have any secrets from a horse.

Cowpoke: Did you see that calf wander up to the silo?
Dude: Yes.
Cowpoke: Do you know what it said?
Dude: No, what?
Cowpoke: Is my fodder in there?

Dude: Is a chicken big enough to eat when it is two weeks old?
Cowbody: Of course not.
Dude: Then how does it stay alive?

Cowhand: I heard they caught the guy who was stealing the pigs. How did they figure out who he was?
Foreman: The pigs squealed.

Waitress at Dude Ranch: "How do you make a milk shake?"
Cowboy: Tickle a cow.

Cowboy: Is there a henweigh in your room?
Dude: What's a henweigh?
Cowboy: Oh, about three pounds.

Dude: What's your horse's name?
Cowboy: I call him Ink.
Dude: Why? He isn't black.
Cowboy: No, but he keeps running out of the pen.

The cowboy went into the general store. "Do you have one-inch nails?" he asked the storekeeper.
"Sure," came the reply.
"It's a good thing," said the cowboy, "'cause my back sure itches!"

Cowpoke: Say, dude, that picture you're painting of a horse is quite good, but it needs a wagon.
Dude: Oh, the horse will draw that.

"Let's go hunting," the cowboy suggested to his two dude friends. They quickly agreed. All day the three tramped through the woods and prairies but all they found was one skinny pheasant.

"We could cook it," said the first dude, "but it isn't big enough for us all."

"Let's just go to bed," said the second dude. "Whoever has the best dream can have the pheasant for breakfast." They all agreed.

The next morning they began to talk about their dreams.

"Well," said the first dude, "I dreamed that I was in a canoe and I paddled from one tropical island to another."

"I dreamed I was a great explorer," said the second dude.

"My," said the cowboy. "I dreamed you were both invited to a king's banquet and didn't want the pheasant, so I got up and ate it."

Foreman to Cowhand: Did you hear about the dude that wore a winter coat to the rodeo?—He heard there would be thousands of fans there.

39

CATS! AND
MORE CATS!

Mrs. Montgomery was driving down her street when Mrs. Beeson's cat ran out in front of her. Mrs. Montgomery hit the brakes but not quickly enough. Feeling quite terrible about the whole thing, she knocked on Mrs. Beeson's door.

"I'm so sorry," said Mrs. Montgomery, holding the injured pet. "I tried to stop, but I'm afraid I've hurt your cat. Please, let me do something to make up for it."

"Of course," replied Mrs. Beeson. "Come back after dark and you can chase mice."

Jean: On my vacation I saw the Catskill Mountains.
Jerry: Really? I thought cats only killed birds.

"Your cat has been staring at the porch light," said Emily. "What is he doing?"

"Oh," said Polly. "He's trying to make a moth bawl."

"Come in and see my new kittens," said Lara.
"How cute," said Darcy, watching them play. "Do you have to get your cats a license?"
"Of course not," said Lara. "They don't know how to drive!"

Joy: What is the difference between a flea and a cat?
Roy: You can always tell. A cat may have fleas, but a flea never has cats.

Roy: Did you find your cat?
Joy: Yes, he was in the refrigerator.
Roy: Is he okay?
Joy: He's more than okay; he's a cool cat.

Beth: Do you think you should take your cat out in the boat like that? You know cats don't really like water.
Jess: I have to take him.
Beth: Why?
Jess: How else will I get to see the catfish?

Beth: My cat likes to drink lemonade.
Jess: Boy, he sure must be a sour puss.

NEW JOKES

The jokes on this page and the next are originals. As far as the compiler can tell, the jokes have never before appeared in print. However, someone, somewhere, may have said something similar.

Joan Embry was touring Washington Zoo. She stopped to watch the pandas in the exhibit. One of the tourists who had seen her on television asked, "When is a panda most likely to come out of his cage?"
"When the door is open," replied Joan.

Tourist (to the park ranger at the campfire nature program): If fish are discovered on Alpha Centauri, what kind of fish do you think they will be?
Ranger: Starfish, of course.

"Did you hear about the man from Gallup?" asked the owner of the fishing resort.
"No," said the fisherman.
"He took a fishing poll," said the owner.

"Look at Ling-Ling. Why is she sweeping a ladybug
into the ant hole?"
"I don't know," said Karen. "Maybe she wants to
see the ant eat 'er."

"I don't know why we have to go to the moon," said
the man from Rahman to his co-pilot. "Someone
has already been there. Let's go to the sun
instead."
"We can't do that," answered the co-pilot. "We'll
burn up."
"Don't be silly," said the man from Rahman. "We'll
go at night!"

"What kind of candy do you find in the vending
machines on the starship?" asked the reporter.
"Milky Ways," said the crew.

Silly: I always wondered how they put the milk in
the Milky Way.
Dilly: With the Big Dipper.

Did you hear about the tailor who wanted to set up a shop on the moon?—He wanted to make space suits.

Kiku: Did you hear what Geela found in the ladies' room on the spaceship?
Meli: No, what?
Kiku: Saturn's rings.

Jed: I heard that some millionaire invited the California Angels to spend a week at his private resort.
Ted: That's right! He wanted to see an Angel fish.

Jim and Tim had just arrived at the fishing resort to spend the week. "I'm sure glad I wasn't here to go swimming last week," said Jim.
"Why?" asked Tim.
"I heard the fishermen talking and they said the fish were really biting last week."

Now It's Your Turn

Words are the chief ingredients of a funny joke. If you mix the words together correctly, you can really stir something up.

Since you have laughed, giggled, tittered, snickered, chuckled, cackled, roared, chortled, and grinned your way through this book to get here, you should have a good feel for what's funny. NOW IT'S YOUR TURN!

Pick up a pencil. You get to write the jokes because this chapter is all yours.

"But I don't know where to start," the new driver said as he crawled behind the steering wheel.

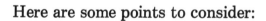

Here are some points to consider:

• A joke is a series of words that sets the reader or listener up and then pulls the rug out from under him with a punch line.

• A punch line is the line that gets the laugh. It's the climax of a humorous story or joke, and it usually comes at the end.

• What is a joke when it isn't a trick you play on someone? It's a wisecrack, a funny story, a play on words known as a pun. It's something that triggers the funny bone and ends in a laugh, giggle, titter, snicker. . . .

• Some people write jokes backwards. They think up a funny line and then they make up a suitable question, or conversation, or story that lets them use the funny line as the punch line and makes the whole thing funny.

For instance:
Punch line: Snow!
Question: What fell last winter but did not get hurt?
Answer: Snow!

• Sample story
  Once there were seven tiny men. They lived together in a cabin in the woods. The tiny men had a kind helper. She helped make their meals. One morning at breakfast one of the men said, "Did you hear anything in the night?"
  "Yes," she said. "Something fell. I wonder what it was."
  "I know," said the smallest tiny man. "But it didn't get hurt."
  "Well?" asked the others. "What was it?"
  (Punch line:) "Snow!"

- Sample conversation joke
  Jed: Did you know that something fell this winter and didn't get broken?
  Ted: Oh, really? What?
  Jed: Snow.

Here are some hints to help YOU get started!

1. Think up a word or phrase that has more than one meaning. It should be possible to use it in an unusual way—a play on words that sound alike and are spelled differently. This word or words will be your punch line.

2. Now pick a subject. What goes with your punch line—camping, dinosaurs, elephants, monsters, modern people, trains? (It could be anything.)

3. Once you have chosen a punch line and a subject, you must decide what kind of joke you want to write—a question joke (usually a riddle), a conversation joke, or a story joke.

4. Now you are ready to set the stage for your punch line. That means you will need to choose characters for a conversation joke or a story and write the joke. That's the hard part! Write the conversation. Narrate the story. Ask the question.

By the way, did you hear about the kids who spent all of their time writing jokes?—They cracked up!